SOUTHWEST WISCONSIN LIBRARY SYSTEM

3 9896 01491 6403

Dodgeville Public Library
139 S. Iowa Street
Dodgeville WI 53533

WITHDRAWN

D1716657

Guest Speaker Program
Kiwanis Club of
City of Dodgeville
Guest Speaker Program

This book is presented to the
Dodgeville Public Library to
recognize the Club's guest speaker:

Presented this *12th* Day of *Aug.* 20 *19*

Reading rocks !

Terry Edwards

Penny Edwards

ULTIMATE
NFL
Road Trip

By Barry Wilner

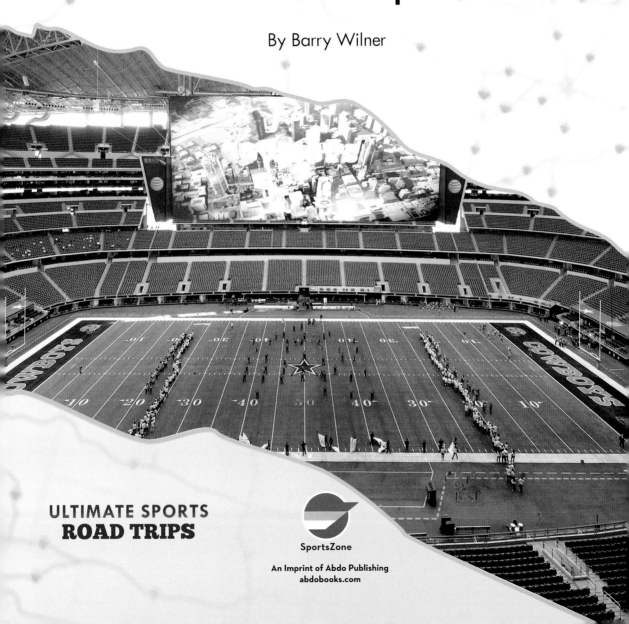

ULTIMATE SPORTS
ROAD TRIPS

SportsZone

An Imprint of Abdo Publishing
abdobooks.com

ABDOBOOKS.COM

Published by Abdo Publishing, a division of ABDO, PO Box 398166, Minneapolis, Minnesota 55439.
Copyright © 2019 by Abdo Consulting Group, Inc. International copyrights reserved in all countries.
No part of this book may be reproduced in any form without written permission from the publisher.
SportsZone™ is a trademark and logo of Abdo Publishing.

Printed in the United States of America, North Mankato, Minnesota
092018
012019

THIS BOOK CONTAINS
RECYCLED MATERIALS

Cover Photo: Ric Tapia/AP Images
Interior Photos: Ric Tapia/AP Images, 1, 30, 35; Aaron M. Sprecher/AP Images, 4–5; Jonathan Daniel/
Getty Images, 7; Matt Patterson/AP Images, 8; Todd Ponath/AP Images, 11; Al Messerschmidt/AP Images,
13; Scott Boehm/AP Images, 14; Akili-Casundria Ramsess/Atlanta Journal & Constitution/AP Images, 17;
David Goldman/AP Images, 18; Logan Bowles/AP Images, 20; Paul Spinelli/AP Images, 23; Alan Diaz/AP
Images, 24; Wilfredo Lee/AP Images, 26–27; Phelan M. Ebenhack/AP Images, 29; Kevin Terrell/AP Images,
32; Todd Rosenberg/AP Images, 36; Shutterstock Images, 39; Ryan Kang/AP Images, 40, 44; Scott Eklund/
AP Images, 42; Frank Mattia/Icon Sportswire/AP Images, 45; Tom Hauck/AP Images, 44

Editor: Bradley Cole
Series Designer: Melissa Martin

Library of Congress Control Number: 2018949192

Publisher's Cataloging-in-Publication Data

Names: Wilner, Barry, author.
Title: Ultimate NFL road trip / by Barry Wilner.
Description: Minneapolis, Minnesota : Abdo Publishing, 2019 | Series: Ultimate sports road trips |
    Includes online resources and index.
Identifiers: ISBN 9781532117558 (lib. bdg.) | ISBN 9781532170416 (ebook)
Subjects: LCSH: Sports arenas--Juvenile literature. | Sports spectators--Juvenile literature. | American
    football--Juvenile literature. | National Football League--Juvenile literature.
Classification: DDC 796.332068--dc23

TABLE OF
CONTENTS

First Down
AND GOAL!

The ultimate professional football road trip will visit the oldest professional football stadium in continuous use and the league's newest stadium. It will celebrate with foam Cheeseheads and Cowboy hats. Fans will wave Terrible Towels and cheer loud enough to be considered the home team's 12th player.

From the brats at famous Green Bay tailgates to Sloppy Joes in Miami and BBQ anything in Kansas City, National Football League (NFL) stadiums have great traditions and great food.

There will be stops in Pittsburgh, Atlanta, Miami, Green Bay, Dallas, Kansas City, and Seattle. There are indoor palaces in Georgia and Texas and outdoor venues in the other cities. They are all great places to watch football. Replays will be on videoboards the size of cruise ships. Oh, and there will be noise—lots of it. Seahawks and Chiefs fans have a rivalry about who can cheer loudest. They have even set noise records. These venues are simply the best places to watch NFL games.

Stadiums can be great because of fans, food, traditions, and how they are built.

1 LAMBEAU
FIELD

Baseball has Fenway Park and Wrigley Field. Auto racing has Indianapolis Motor Speedway and Daytona International Speedway. Golf has St. Andrews and Augusta National. For pro football, the place to be is Lambeau Field, the first football-only stadium built in the NFL.

Lambeau, home of the Green Bay Packers, is located in the smallest city to host an American professional sports team (population just over 100,000). In spite of that, it has played a huge role in the history of the NFL. Some of football's greatest players and teams have called it home. The coach for whom the Super Bowl trophy is named, Vince Lombardi, won seven straight championships in nine total seasons at the helm. That run ended with Packers victories in the first two Super Bowls.

Located in the northern reaches of Wisconsin, Green Bay is the coldest city in the NFL. But that doesn't stop the hardy fans, who are called *Cheeseheads* for the yellow foam hats they sometimes

LAMBEAU FIELD

Green Bay, Wisconsin

Date Opened: September 29, 1957
Capacity: 81,441
Home Team: Green Bay Packers

wear. Every seat is filled, no matter how far the temperatures drop. They even showed up for the Ice Bowl.

On the last day of 1967, the Dallas Cowboys came to Lambeau for the NFL title game. That morning when the Dallas players looked out their hotel rooms, they couldn't see through the ice caked

 In chilly Wisconsin, the Packers often play in cold and snowy conditions.

on their windows. The thermometer read minus-13 degrees Fahrenheit (-25°C). The wind chill reached minus-48 degrees Fahrenheit (-44°C). The game still took place.

Even with the extreme cold, the visitors were winning 17–14 late in the game. But Hall of Fame quarterback Bart Starr marched the Packers 67 yards to the Dallas 1-yard line. Lombardi could have ordered a tying field goal in the final seconds. But no one wanted to stay on the frozen field for overtime. The heating coils beneath the field had failed in the freezing temperatures. The play was a run from the fullback, but Starr was afraid the fullback wouldn't be able to get traction on the frozen field. So Lombardi called for a quarterback sneak. Starr surged into the end zone for the win.

The stadium is named for Curly Lambeau, a Hall of Fame coach for the Packers from 1919 to 1949. It was originally called City Stadium but was renamed for Lambeau in 1965, after he died.

No trip to Lambeau would be complete without visiting the Packers Hall of Fame. It sits on the main floor of the stadium's atrium. The thrills for fans include interactive displays and film and photos of the greatest moments in team history. It also holds a replica of Lombardi's office from the 1960s.

Perhaps the coolest attraction is seeing the best players ever to suit up for Green Bay describing famous games. Select highlights from those games are cued up on touch screens at each display.

The trophy case is definitely a must-see. The Packers have won 13 NFL titles including four Super Bowls. Packers players have also won the NFL Most Valuable Player Award 10 times.

FUN FACT

It cost only $960,000 to build the venue in 1957, and all loans were paid off by 1978. It's estimated a similar stadium would cost more than $1 billion to build today.

During a game a Packer might try a Lambeau Leap after scoring a touchdown. Being swallowed up by fans in the front row dressed in green and gold is a grand Lambeau tradition.

Lambeau Field also has some of the best tailgating in the NFL. Packers fans are crazy about their famed Wisconsin bratwurst and cheese curds. And fans who don't get their fill in the parking lot can enjoy a meal at one of Lambeau's three restaurants. One is open year-round.

 After touchdowns at Lambeau Field, players leap into the stands to celebrate with fans.

HEINZ
FIELD

One of the first things people notice about attending a Steelers game at Heinz Field is the Terrible Towels. The gold cloths have become a major part of the Steelers experience. They date back to the championship days of the "Steel Curtain," the name given to the team's dominant defensive line in the 1970s. Fans begin waving them during warmups, and by kickoff the stadium is full and the noise is loud.

Heinz Field is a horseshoe-style stadium with the south end open, so fans can see the Pittsburgh skyline. Behind those seats is a 27-by-96-foot (8-by-29-m) videoboard. On each side of the board is a giant neon ketchup bottle. It "pours" onto the screen whenever the Steelers get inside the opponents' 20-yard line, also known as the red zone.

FUN FACT

How tough is it to get a ticket to a Steelers game? Every home game has been a sellout since 1972, when the team played in Three Rivers Stadium, next to where Heinz Field now sits.

HEINZ FIELD

Pittsburgh, Pennsylvania

Date Opened: August 25, 2001
Capacity: 65,500
Home Team: Pittsburgh Steelers

Around the stadium, 60 murals were painted by local high school art students to show what football means to them. Another must at Heinz Field is eating a sandwich from Primanti Brothers. One is big enough to serve as lunch and dinner. And to get a feel for Steelers and Pittsburgh sports history, fans can check out the

 Steelers fans show up to Heinz Field to support their team every game.

Great Hall on the east side of the stadium. It is set up like a football field and even has yard stripes. It contains mementos, trophies, interactive displays, and even a food court. There is so much to see and do at the Great Hall that it is a great way to kick off any visit to Heinz Field.

Through their five championships, there have been plenty of big moments in Pittsburgh. Heinz Field has seen some of the craziest moments in Steelers history. On January 18, 2009, safety Troy Polamalu returned an interception 40 yards for a touchdown to clinch a 23–14 victory over rival Baltimore. Two weeks later, Pittsburgh won its sixth Super Bowl title.

FUN FACT

Because the first and third games were away and the second game was rescheduled, Heinz Field didn't host its first regular-season game until October 7, 2001. The Steelers went 7–1 at home during that regular season.

3 MERCEDES-BENZ
STADIUM

The home of the Atlanta Falcons is one of the league's newest venues. Mercedes-Benz Stadium has all the state-of-the-art comforts a fan could wish for. The amenities start with the amazing videoboard. At 63,000 square feet (5,800 sq m) of screen, the "Halo Board" is impossible to ignore. It is a 58-foot (18-m) tall ring that sits in the opening of the stadium's roof and provides scores, replays, and stats to fans in every direction. It is the first circular video board ever built.

The roof opens in multiple pieces—no other NFL stadium has anything like it. It covers seats that are 21 inches (53 cm) wide, 2 inches (5 cm) wider than the seats in the Georgia Dome, the stadium next door that Mercedes-Benz Stadium replaced.

The "Window to the City" is a glass wall that gives a great view of Atlanta while bringing natural light into the building without interrupting the game. With 2,000 TV screens spread throughout the concourses, it's unlikely fans will miss any plays even when in line for concessions. Falcons owner Arthur Blank thought

MERCEDES-BENZ STADIUM

Atlanta, Georgia

Date Opened: August 26, 2017
Capacity: 71,000
Home Team: Atlanta Falcons

of everything. Fans can even walk all the way around the stadium to catch the game from any angle. Most stadiums are broken up into sections or decks, but not Mercedes-Benz Stadium. The Falcons' home might be the nicest stadium for the fans in the whole league. It may even be the nicest stadium for fans in the whole world.

And don't forget the food. Blank insisted on fan-friendly prices. Pizza slices are $3, whereas soda and hot dogs are $2. For something more southern, the cheddarwurst corn dog at Golden Brown and Delicious is a bargain for $8. It even has smoked ketchup on it.

Savannah College of Art and Design curated an art exhibit for the stadium. It gathered one of the finest art collections in American sports, including original art by Atlanta artists and other commissioned works. The exhibit has paintings, sculptures,

FUN FACT
The Halo Board isn't the only large screen in the Mercedes-Benz Stadium. There's a 100-foot (30-m) mega column that is covered in LCD displays on three sides.

Designed to be modern and to give the ultimate fan experience, Mercedes-Benz Stadium looks like no other stadium.

 The Atlanta Falcons moved into their new stadium in 2017.

photographs, drawings, and digital art installations. The artwork is one more way the stadium is focused on the fan experience.

Of course, part of a great fan experience is leaving the game with the win. The Falcons' first home opener in Mercedes-Benz Stadium was against Green Bay in Week 2 of the 2017 season. It was a nationally televised game. Atlanta built a 31–7 lead before winning 34–23, getting their new building off to a great start.

The dome provides the climate-controlled environment that most quarterbacks love. Atlanta's Matt Ryan threw for 252 yards in the opener. They went on to finish 5-3 at home in their first year in their new stadium.

FUN FACT

Soccer has been as popular as football at Mercedes-Benz Stadium. The Atlanta United of Major League Soccer often draw crowds as big as the Falcons get—more than 70,000 fans.

4 HARD ROCK STADIUM

The Hard Rock Stadium has hosted five Super Bowls since it opened in 1987. It was Joe Robbie Stadium then, named for the former owner of the Miami Dolphins. The NFL returns for the south Florida weather but also considers the venue a Super Bowl-caliber stadium. Just as important as the weather, Hard Rock Stadium is great for a championship game. Improvements to the stadium in 2016 included a remodel of the club level and 147 suites. Party terraces were added in the four corners of the venue. High-end seating was put in to give the feel of watching the game from a yacht. The 14 four-person boxes behind the east end zone at field level include a private club serving food and beverages. At midfield is the 72 Club, named for the 1972 Dolphins that went 17–0 and won the NFL title. The club has wider seats that are double padded and offer more leg room than regular seats.

More than $500 million was spent on the three-year project. Most notable was the redesign of the roof. Miami can be a

HARD ROCK STADIUM

Miami Gardens, Florida

Date Opened: August 16, 1987
Capacity: 64,767
Home Team: Miami Dolphins

 In sunny Miami, it is important to give as many fans as possible shade during games.

hot place to watch football. Dolphins owner Stephen Ross

wanted most of the fans to have seats that were covered.

The roof or canopy, with a style similar to European soccer

arenas, shelters 92 percent of the fans from the sun or rain.

Studies have shown the temperature in the shade can be

30 degrees Fahrenheit (-17°C) cooler at times.

The canopy is held up by four towers called spires, one in each corner of the stadium to keep up the canopy. Hurricane Irma tested the strength of the design when it hit south Florida in 2017. But the towers held firm against wind gusts that reached 99 miles per hour (160 km/h). The only losses were a section of roof panels and some trees.

Fans don't go to Hard Rock Stadium to just watch the Dolphins, even if the team has some of the coolest jerseys and helmets in sports. They want the total experience and food is a major part. The Dolphins brought in celebrity chef David Chang in 2017 to help update the menu. If you want breakfast before the game, try O-B House. It features three types of pancakes: plain, blueberry, and andouille sausage and corn.

More in the mood for lunch? Head to Cafe Versailles, which has a terrific Cuban sandwich. Or try conch fritters

FUN FACT

How many names has the stadium had since opening in 1987? Nine.

- Joe Robbie Stadium (1987)
- Pro Player Park (1996)
- Pro Player Stadium (1996)
- Dolphins Stadium (2005)
- Dolphin Stadium (2006)
- Land Shark Stadium (2009)
- Sun Life Stadium (2010)
- New Miami Stadium (2016)
- Hard Rock Stadium (2017)

 Hard Rock Stadium hosts the Miami Dolphins and the University of Miami.

straight out of Key West at Sloppy Joe's. The food at Hard Rock

Stadium is top notch. Surprisingly, given the name of the place,

there's no Hard Rock Cafe at the stadium. But that's about the only

luxury missing at Hard Rock Stadium.

To honor their Hall of Fame quarterback, the team retired Dan Marino's No. 13 jersey on September 17, 2000. It later installed a life-size bronze statue of Marino and renamed Stadium Street to Dan Marino Boulevard.

AT&T
STADIUM

Some call it the Palace in Dallas. Others have named it Jerry's World after Cowboys owner Jerry Jones. AT&T Stadium is a must-see for any NFL fan, even when it isn't hosting a game. There are five different tours to take of the 100,000-seat venue that give fans a close-up view of the field, a collection of contemporary art, and the interview room.

When driving to the game, AT&T Stadium can be seen from miles away. It's located in Arlington, Texas, which is between Fort Worth and Dallas. On clear days, it's easy to spot the colossal stadium from either city. Other entertainment options nearby include Texas Rangers baseball, River Legacy Park on the Trinity River—a great place for a picnic—and the Six Flags Over Texas amusement park.

There isn't as much room for tailgating here as at other NFL venues, and that's by design. The Cowboys want visitors to come

AT&T STADIUM

Arlington, Texas

Date Opened: May 27, 2009
Capacity: 100,000
Home Team: Dallas Cowboys

through the gates early, so they offer two stages for musical acts located on plazas on opposite sides of the stadium.

Inside the stadium feels like another world. High above the famous star at midfield is a massive videoboard. At 180 feet by

 AT&T Stadium has hosted all kinds of sporting events and concerts.

72 feet (55 m by 22 m) it was the largest of its kind when the stadium opened. Fans in the upper decks might end up watching more of the game on the board than on the field.

A beautiful art collection is spread throughout the building, not something found in most football stadiums. Pregame entertainment is provided by the Dallas Cowboys Drum Line, the Rhythm & Blues Dancers, motorcycle-riding team mascot Rowdy, and the world-famous Dallas Cowboys Cheerleaders.

FUN FACT

How big is AT&T Stadium? The entire Statue of Liberty and its base could fit inside, even with the roof closed.

Perhaps the best seats in the stadium are the lower club seats, adjacent to where the players walk to get onto the field. You just might get a high-five from a player. Standing-room tickets are available in both the east and west end zone. Whether fans are in need of last-second tickets or cheaper admission, these spots provide access to Jerry's World on a budget.

Fan favorites at the concession stands include the catfish po-boy sandwich and the Texas Frito pie (chili, cheese, and corn chips). They have a burger topped with fried macaroni and cheese

with a crushed-Fritos crust. It can even be dipped in Buffalo sauce. It comes with a Roma tomato, romaine, and garlic aioli. And there are more normal dishes such as gluten-free turkey sandwiches or the classic peanut butter and jelly sandwich.

FUN FACT

AT&T Stadium hosted the 2018 NFL Draft, the first time the NFL held its draft of college players in a team's stadium.

AT&T Stadium also holds children's birthday parties. It hosts all kinds of other sporting events as well. The stadium was the site of the 2010 NBA All-Star Game, numerous boxing matches, and WrestleMania 32. Although the stadium is one of the newest in the NFL, it has already hosted a Super Bowl. On February 6, 2011, the Green Bay Packers beat the Pittsburgh Steelers 31–25 before 103,219 fans in Super Bowl XLV.

Approximately 100,000 fans fill AT&T Stadium on game day.

 Arrowhead Stadium has been the home of the Chiefs since 1972.

spaces can hold up to 1,000 guests. The smells of beef, pork, and chicken are in the air.

Inside the stadium, fans fill up on a local favorite, the Arrowhead Biscuit: pancakes, fried egg, cheese, bacon, and hash browns. After all, it takes a lot of fuel to make that much noise.

Developers had planned for a rolling roof when Arrowhead Stadium was designed. If it had been built, it would have been the first covered stadium in the NFL. That would have made Arrowhead even louder. However, the Chiefs found it would cost too much and delay the entire project, so the roof was scrapped.

FUN FACT

Baseball fans can walk from Arrowhead Stadium across the parking lot to watch a Kansas City Royals game next door in Kauffman Stadium. Both venues are part of the Truman Sports Complex.

The football team has given its fans plenty of reasons to get loud through the years. Even late in his career, Hall of Fame quarterback Joe Montana was leading game-winning drives. He won his final home playoff game here. He led Kansas City to a 27–24 victory over Pittsburgh in a wild-card game in the 1993 season. Montana threw for 276 yards and a touchdown that forced overtime.

7 CENTURYLINK FIELD

enturyLink Field is the home of the Seattle Seahawks. And it is loud. It might be hard to believe that an outdoor venue could produce more noise than an indoor or domed stadium. But this one can. Seattle fans have set multiple records for the loudest roar in a sports stadium.

Seahawks fans set a noise record on December 2, 2013. An official from Guinness World Records measured 137.6 decibels in a Monday night win against the New Orleans Saints. A jet engine at 100 feet (30 m) above the ground is approximately 140 decibels. The record was later claimed by Kansas City, but the noise in Seattle affects games. Visiting players frequently mention the noise in their postgame interviews.

Seahawks fans cheer and boo loudly, for sure. But it's more than that. Nearly 70 percent of the almost 72,000 seats are under a roof. The noise bounces off the coverings and stays in the building.

CENTURYLINK FIELD

Seattle, Washington

Date Opened: August 10, 2002
Capacity: 72,000
Home Team: Seattle Seahawks

Those roofs are angled and made of metal and concrete. They reflect the sound and keep it in the stadium.

The seats are closer to the field than in most NFL stadiums, which also helps retain noise. It all makes for a great home-field

 CenturyLink Field provides one of the NFL's best home-field advantages.

advantage for the Seahawks. Seattle's "Legion of Boom" defense has definitely benefitted from the noisy fans. The noise makes it hard for visiting offenses to communicate and even hear the quarterback hike the ball.

A trip to CenturyLink Field is a good idea for other reasons, too. In many areas of the stadium, fans can order food from their seats on the stadium's Wi-Fi, never missing any action. The Seahawks offer dishes from four different local restaurants each game. The chicken and waffles from Ezell's are suitable for breakfast, lunch, or dinner. And Seattle Dogs even sells vegan frankfurters.

Just before kickoff, the 12th Man goes into action. The 12th Man—a reference to the fans who cheer so loudly—is represented by a celebrity who raises a giant flag before every game. Sometimes a former Seahawks great raises it. Maybe a well-known fan or perhaps even team owner Paul Allen raises it. When the 12 flag goes up,

FUN FACT

Near CenturyLink Field is Touchdown City, a free park with football-themed activities perfect for kids (and adults). Fans don't even need a ticket to the Seahawks game to go and enjoy the place.

the noise peaks and you know how CenturyLink Field earned its reputation.

A big moment for the 12th Man came in the 2014 NFC Championship Game. Behind great performances from young quarterback Russell Wilson and running back Marshawn Lynch, the Seahawks beat the rival San Francisco 49ers 23–17 to reach Super Bowl XLVIII. Having the top defense didn't hurt either. Two weeks later they beat the Denver Broncos 43–8 for their first NFL title.

With the fans, noise, food, and technology, Seattle's CenturyLink Field is one of the greatest places to watch football. It certainly has earned its spot in the ultimate football road trip.

FUN FACT

It's not only Seahawks fans who rock the building to record numbers. Folks attending Seattle Sounders soccer games are so loud it makes CenturyLink the most ear-ringing stadium in Major League Soccer.

Seahawks fans get pumped for the appearance of the 12th Man flag.

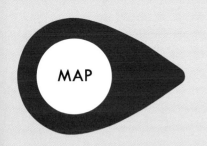

MAP

1. **Lambeau Field.** Green Bay, Wisconsin
2. **Heinz Field.** Pittsburgh, Pennsylvania
3. **Mercedes-Benz Stadium.** Atlanta, Georgia

4. **Hard Rock Stadium.** Miami Gardens, Florida
5. **AT&T Stadium.** Arlington, Texas
6. **Arrowhead Stadium.** Kansas City, Missouri
7. **CenturyLink Field.** Seattle, Washington

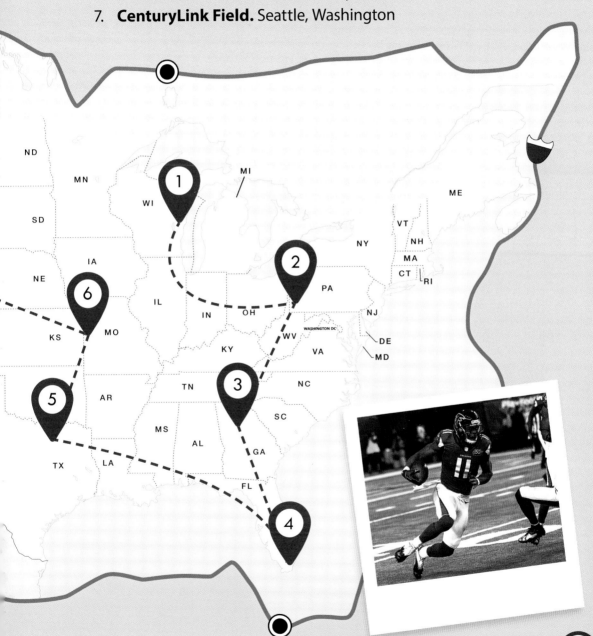

Glossary

atrium

An open-roofed entrance hall or central court.

Cheesehead

A yellow foam "hat" shaped like a piece of cheese and worn by Packers fans; also a nickname for a Packers fan.

concessions

A space within certain venues for a business or service, often preparing food.

Hall of Fame

The highest honor a player can get when his career is over.

Ice Bowl

The nickname given to the 1967 NFL Championship Game, played in frigid temperatures at Green Bay's Lambeau Field.

premium

Special or high-end.

spire

A cone-shaped or pyramid-shaped tower.

suite

A separate room or set of rooms.

tailgating

A social gathering outside a stadium, often with food served from the back of a parked vehicle.

ultimate

The very best or the very last.

More Information

BOOKS

Lowell, Barbara. *Engineering AT&T Stadium*. Minneapolis, MN: Abdo Publishing, 2018.

Martin, Brett S. *STEM in Football*. Minneapolis, MN: Abdo Publishing, 2018.

Wilner, Barry. *Total Football*. Minneapolis, MN: Abdo Publishing, 2017.

Online Resources

Booklinks
NONFICTION NETWORK
FREE! ONLINE NONFICTION RESOURCES

To learn more about NFL stadiums, visit **abdobooklinks.com**. These links are routinely monitored and updated to provide the most current information available.

Index

About the Author

Barry Wilner has been a sports writer for the Associated Press (AP) since 1976 and currently is the AP's NFL Writer. He has written more than five dozen books and also teaches communications at Manhattanville College. Barry lives in Garnerville, New York.